GODDESS

Meditative Coloring Book 7

Adult coloring for relaxation, stress reduction, meditation, spiritual connection, prayer, centering, healing, and coming into your deep true self; ages 9 to 109

Aliyah Schick

Books by Aliyah Schick

- Angels Meditative Coloring Book 1
- Crosses Meditative Coloring Book 2
- Ancient Symbols Meditative Coloring Book 3
- Hearts Meditative Coloring Book 4
- Labyrinths Meditative Coloring Book 5
- OM Meditative Coloring Book 6
- Goddess Meditative Coloring Book 7

- Judaica Jewish Coloring Book for Grown Ups
- Chai Jewish Coloring Book for Grown Ups
- Alefbet Jewish Coloring Book for Grown Ups
- Star of David Jewish Coloring Book for Grown Ups

- The Labyrinth Guided Journal, A Year in the Labyrinth
- Mary Magdalene's Words:
  Two Women's Spiritual Journey,
  Both Truth and Fiction, Both Ancient and Now.
- The Mary Magdalene Book: Mary Magdalene Speaks,
  Her Story and Her Message
- Finally, a Book of Poetry by Aliyah Schick

ISBN: 978-0-9882731-3-9

www.MeditativeColoring.com

Table of Contents

2 The Goddess

7 More

8 Symbols

10 Suggestions for How to Use This Book

11 Meditation

12 About the Artist/Author

13 The Drawings

86 The Meditative Coloring Books

Dedicated to
joyful discovery and
exploration
of our
sacred feminine.

Goddess Celebration

Ancient people all around the world celebrated and worshipped the sacred feminine, the Great Mother Goddess, and Her life-giving abilities for 30,000 years in prehistoric times. Overwhelming archeological evidence of Goddess worship dates from the prehistoric Upper Paleolithic through the Neolithic Age, that is from about 35,000 B.C.E. until about 4000 B.C.E.

The Goddess religion was a way of life in which everything was sacred. She gave birth to everything, and She was the life force within everything. Beliefs and practices were inspired by nature, by the movements of the sun, moon, and stars, and by the cycles of the seasons. Worship was every day here and now, holistic, visceral and sensual, all about earth, body, and nature, and embracing all phases of life: fertility, birth, death, and renewal.

The Paleolithic

Throughout the Paleolithic Era, until nearly 8,000 B.C.E., glaciers came far down into Europe and North America and climates all over the earth were much colder than they are now. Humans were hunter-gatherers, constantly on the move following migrating animal herds and searching for food.

Most of what we have learned about Goddess worship in Paleolithic times comes from two sources. The first source, artifacts from daily life, are found in the accumulated layers of the floors of living spaces near the openings of caves. Small, portable figures and decorated amulets and beads were carved from stone, bone or antler or shaped from clay. Most of the figures are clearly female, with minimized faces, arms, and legs, emphasizing reproductive parts. They often have wide hips symbolizing excellent child-bearing abilities, or the large, drooping breasts and heavy hips of a woman who has had children. The figurines celebrate fertility, birthing, nurturing, and the life force that is powerful, present, and accessible in the Goddess.

The other source is paintings on walls of caves used for sacred ritual, deep in the earth at the ends of long, treacherous tunnels. Just getting there was a spiritual journey into the dark, into the source of life, into the depths of creation. It must have been a powerful experience to be in those caves, within the womb of the Great Mother, participating in spiritual ceremonies.

Paleolithic cave paintings illustrate nature, rituals, self-decoration, music, and tools, They tend to be symbolic rather than realistic, which strongly suggests sacred ritual. Paints were made from minerals, ochres, burnt bone meal, and charcoal mixed into water, blood, animal fats, and tree saps.

The Neolithic

Glaciers gradually retreated from about 11,000 to 8000 B.C.E. This allowed climates to stabilize and the land to warm. Abundant food enabled change from nomadic tribes to settled life, the beginnings of farming, some domestication of animals, and a new relationship with nature.

During the Neolithic period, from about 7,000 to 4,000 B.C.E., much of life as we know it began to develop: villages, agriculture, trade, communication, cultural exchange, government, more formal religion and Goddess shrines, weaving, pottery, stone working, and eventually metalworking for tools and ornaments. Artisan's workshops were often attached to shrines, suggesting they worked in service to the Goddess.

Tens of thousands of small Neolithic sculptures have survived, made of stone, bone, clay and even some of copper and gold. Unlike the earlier faceless figurines, these have faces and features, with emphasis on eyes. They have large, bountiful bodies, often pregnant or lactating. Some are squatting and giving birth. In among the many female figures are some animals, too, representing qualities needed for survival. We also have found a great many decorated ritual vessels, wall paintings, altars, and shines to the Goddess. All represent fertility, birthing, and regeneration.

The Ice Age's sacred female evolved into the Great Goddess of Neolithic culture, the pregnant grain goddess, whose body is the landscape's sacred mountains, hills, rivers, and caves.

War Against the Goddess

Judeo-Christian scriptures relate how the new male God in about 2000 B.C.E. ordered the Hebrews to destroy whole populations of "idol worshippers." Many of those victims were followers of the old Goddess religions. Christians eventually took over the annihilation with the Crusades, the Inquisition, and centuries of worldwide efforts to conquer and convert. The last Goddess temple closed in the fifth century C.E., and remnants of the sacred feminine went into hiding.

The war against celebration of the sacred feminine decimated a whole way of living. The supreme sacred as male translates as "power over," givng humans the right to dominate and use up nature, and male the right to dominate female. We have lost the honoring of the essence of life in every being, respect and appreciation for nature, holding the land as sacred, and celebration of fertility and renewal. Anything considered feminine or female, i.e. anything heart-centered, soulful, fertile, soft, ripe, erotic, or dark, is instead depicted at best as frivolous and foolish, and often as dangerous, evil, and to be feared.

And yet, this doesn't mean the sacred feminine has ceased to exist, or that people have lost their instinctive understanding of its meaning and significance. All through the centuries since Goddess celebration was suppressed, people have preserved what they could of it within the new religions. We can easily find Her in Greek and Roman goddesses, in the Shekinah in Judaism and Mother Mary in Catholicism. In recent times we are seeing a worldwide revival of appreciation for nature, simplicity, mindfulness, meaningfulness, and clarity, along with a growing desire to honor intuition, right-brain knowing, and deep connection.

The sacred feminine is built into all of life and all of us, female and male alike, and it is awakening again. We have an opportunity now to nurture and revive this long-abandoned side of conscious living, and bring ourselves and our societies into a more sustainable balance.

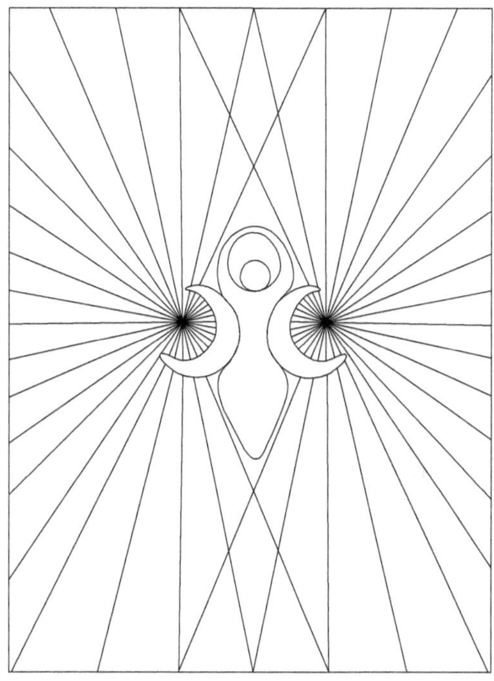

More

A few of the many books to explore for more on the sacred feminine:

- Merlin Stone, *When God Was a Woman*
- Riane Eisler, *The Chalice and the Blade: Our History, Our Future*
- Elinor Gadon, *The Once & Future Goddess: a Sweeping Visual Chronicle of the Sacred Female and Her Reemergence in the Cultural Mythology of Our Time*
- Monica Sjoo & Barbara Mor, *The Great Cosmic Mother: Rediscovering the Religion of the Earth*
- Sharon Paice MacLeod, *The Divine Feminine in Ancient Europe: Goddesses, Sacred Women and the Origins of Western Culture*
- Irene Diamond & Gloria Feman Orenstein editors, *Reweaving the World: the Emergence of Ecofeminism*
- Carol P. Christ, *Rebirth of the Goddess: Finding Meaning in Feminist Spirituality*
- Sue Monk Kidd, *The Dance of the Dissident Daughter*
- Sherry Ruth Anderson & Patricia Hopkins, *The Feminine Face of God, The Unfolding of the Sacred in Women*
- Sera Beak, *Red Hot and Holy, A Heretic's Love Story*

Symbols

Art and artifacts recovered from archeological exploration at Paleolithic and Neolithic sites carry the beliefs and meaning and significance of the sacred feminine in the lives of our Stone Age ancestors. Many of the same images and symbols show up in ancient sites all over the world. How is this possible? Did these symbols arise out of some inherent, universal human understanding? Similar worldwide coherences show up in languages, also.

In some ways art hasn't changed much in these 40,000 years of human expression. Our biology is the same. We create, see, and respond to shape, pattern, texture, dimension, and color in ways very similar to our ancestors. This allows us to make some good guesses about the meaning and significance of ancient art and symbols, and there is plenty of debate.

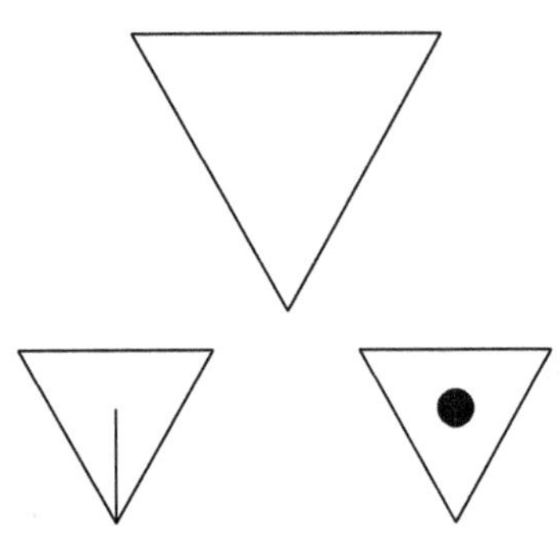

One widely used prehistoric image for the sacred feminine is the downward pointing triangle as a symbol for female genitals, fertility, reproduction, and giving of life. It is both representational and abstract. Some triangles have a line toward the bottom, and some are even more explicit. Some have a dot in the center indicating the seed of life. This triangle is still used in Hindu sacred art to represent the life force as female.

Another symbol for the vulva and the giving of life is a circle with a radius line down from the center.

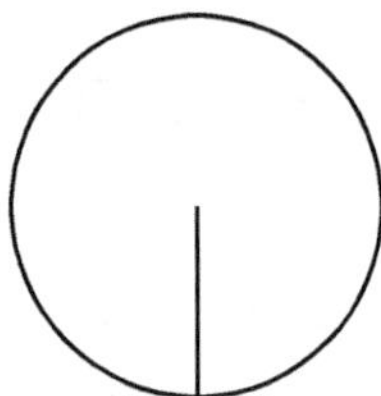

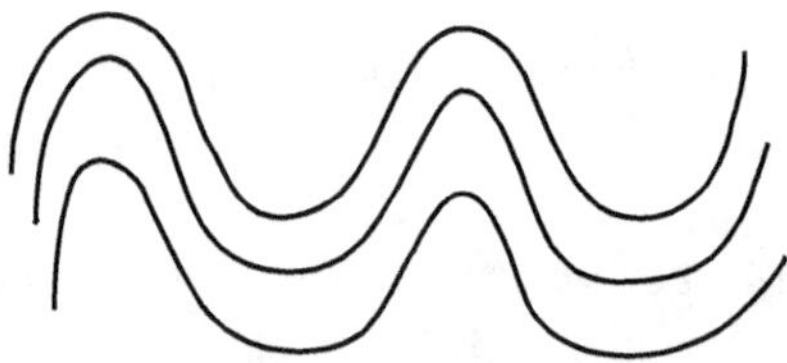

Lines meandering in parallel patterns found on ritual objects and cave walls represent water, rain, birth waters, or mother's milk, all essential elements and sustainers of life.

Spirals are thought to indicate motion, the movement of life, or going upward or downward.

A labyrinth symbolizes going deeper as you enter the passage and find your way to the Mother's womb, then experience rebirth as you come back out.

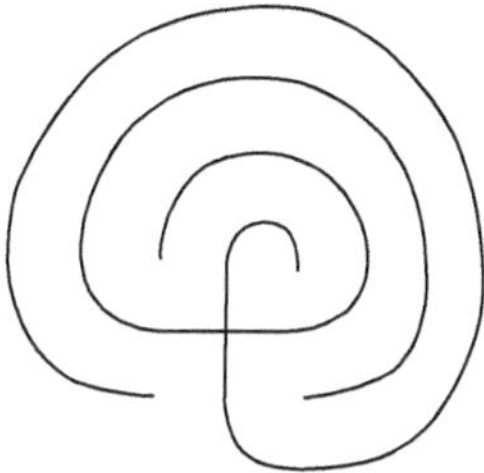

Sets of three show up in many forms within ancient images: three interlocking crescents or circles or curves or spirals. They represent the three aspects of the Triple Goddess: maiden, mother, and crone; the cycle of life: fertility, birth, and death; three worlds: sky, earth, and underworld; and three phases of the moon: waxing, full, and waning.

Even the most simple images found on Paleolithic and Neolithic artifacts and walls were not merely decorative. As with more recent aboriginal people, decoration had a sacred function. The female figures and cave paintings were not just about fertility, or child birth, or successful hunts. They represented the life force that enlivens all existence. Sexual symbolism was not erotic. It was about the sacred force of nature. The Goddess of prehistoric times was both the sacred female and sacred nature. She gave life and sustained it. She was the life force in all that is.

Suggestions for How to Use This Book

Use this ***Goddess Meditative Coloring Book*** to spend time immersed in the sacred feminine, with prayer, relaxation, healing, centering, and for coming into your deep, true self. You may simply wish to experience the images in quiet contemplation. Or, focus on a chant or affirmation as you work with colors. Or, ask for understanding regarding an issue you are dealing with. Or, ask for a clearer sense of some aspect of yourself and how it serves you. You may wish to learn about your path or purpose in this lifetime.

Open your heart and your mind. Pay attention to impressions and ideas, feelings, intuition, and messages. They may very well be exactly what you need to hear.

Tools

Choose your favorite coloring tools, or you might like to gather a variety of pens, crayons, colored pencils, chalk, oil pastels, markers, glitter pens, paints, etc. You may want to place a blank sheet of paper behind the page so ink or paint does not go through.

Music

Consider playing a recording of soft instrumental background music, or try listening to Goddess chants, such as *From the Goddess* or *Ancient Mother* by On Wings of Song.

Silence

You may prefer quiet, so that all your attention focuses on what you are doing. Emptiness can give rise to profound experience.

Nature

A favorite spot outdoors can provide just the right environment for connecting with your sacred feminine. Beach, woods, backyard, porch, treehouse, mountain top, stream, pond, park, etc.

Meditation

You may like to meditate first, and then begin working with the colors. Try any of the many ways of meditation, or simply be with your breath for a few minutes, following it in and out. Or, you may wish to try the guided meditation on the next page. Read it silently or out loud, slowly, pausing to draw in each breath.

Meditation

Take in a breath… and on the exhale release the day's happenings, settling into this peaceful time of creative, spiritual connection.

Take in a breath… and on the exhale let go of worries and troubles and burdens. You can pick them up again later if you need to.

Take in a breath… and on the exhale come into the center of your Self. From there drop a line down through your body, through the chair and the floor and into the earth. Through soil and sand and stone, through coal and underground stream, and minerals and precious metals. Down through all the colors and textures and densities of the earth, down into the hot magma at this planet's core. Down to the very center of the earth, to the Heart of the Mother. Tie your line there. Anchor yourself there.

Take in a breath… and on the exhale extend your line up from your center, through your body and out the crown of your head, up through the ceiling, the roof, and into the sky. Past clouds and wind and thinning gases, out through the atmosphere and into space. Past the sun and galaxy and stars and universe, out to the depths of the Source of All That Is. Feel your connection there. You are part of the great cosmos. You are one with all being.

Take in a breath… and on the exhale return to the drawing before you and ask that you be open to receiving guidance and understanding as you spend time with it. Know that there are no mistakes, only new choices and combinations and patterns that suggest new perception at an other-than-conscious level. Or that remind us of something that can now be released. Or that create an opening to new possibilities.

Take in a breath… and on the exhale release "shoulds" and rules and expectations. Let go and open to new possibilities.

Now, begin by picking up whatever color catches your attention.

About the Artist

Aliyah Schick has been an artist all of her life. After Peace Corps in the Andes Mountains of South America, she studied art full time for four years, then created and sold pottery and ceramic art pieces for many years. Later Aliyah worked in fiber and fabric, making soft sculptural wall pieces and art quilts, then fabric dolls designed to carry healing energy. Now she draws and paints, and she writes poems and prose.

At the heart of all this, Aliyah's real work is healing. She is a skilled and dynamic deep energetic healer. Her work in the multidimensional layers and patterns of the auric field is powerful and effective. The ***Sacred Imprints***™ drawings, paintings, poetry, and writings, and the ***Meditative Coloring***™ ***Books*** emerged as new expressions of Aliyah's healing work. Experiencing these drawings serves to remind us who we are, where we come from, and why we are here.

Aliyah lives and works in the beautiful Blue Ridge Mountains of North Carolina, where the energy of the earth is easily accessible, ancient, motherly, and obvious. A place where people speak with familiarity and reverence of the land and spirit, and where the sacred comes to sit with us on the porch to share the afternoon sun.

www.AliyahSchick.com

The Drawings

Opposite each drawing is a blank page labeled Meditative Impressions. Use these pages to catch and keep hold of your thoughts, wishes, intentions, affirmations, prayers, poems, memories, notes, drawings, or whatever comes to you as you explore coloring with this book. Make it yours.

Meditative Impressions

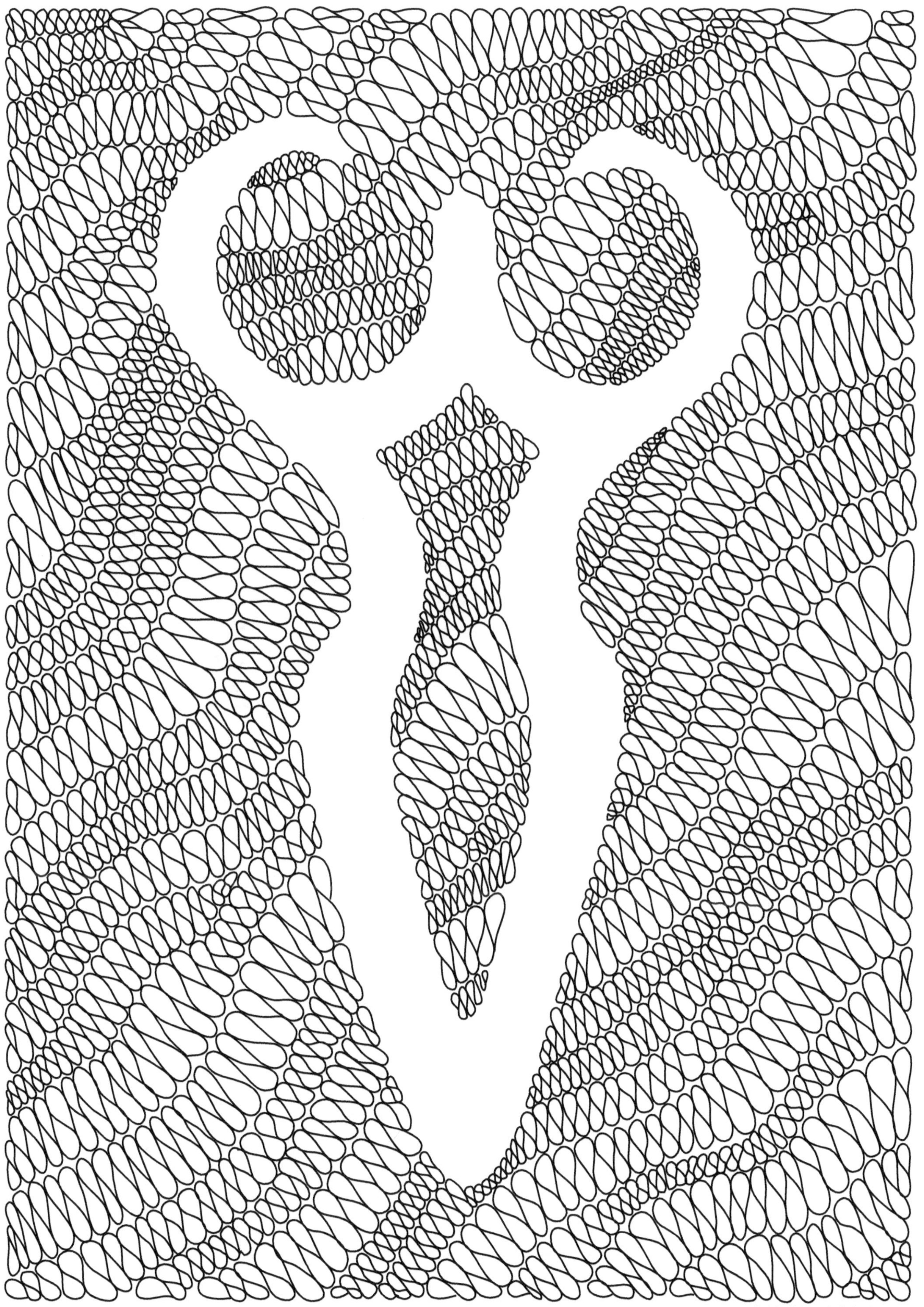

Meditative Impressions

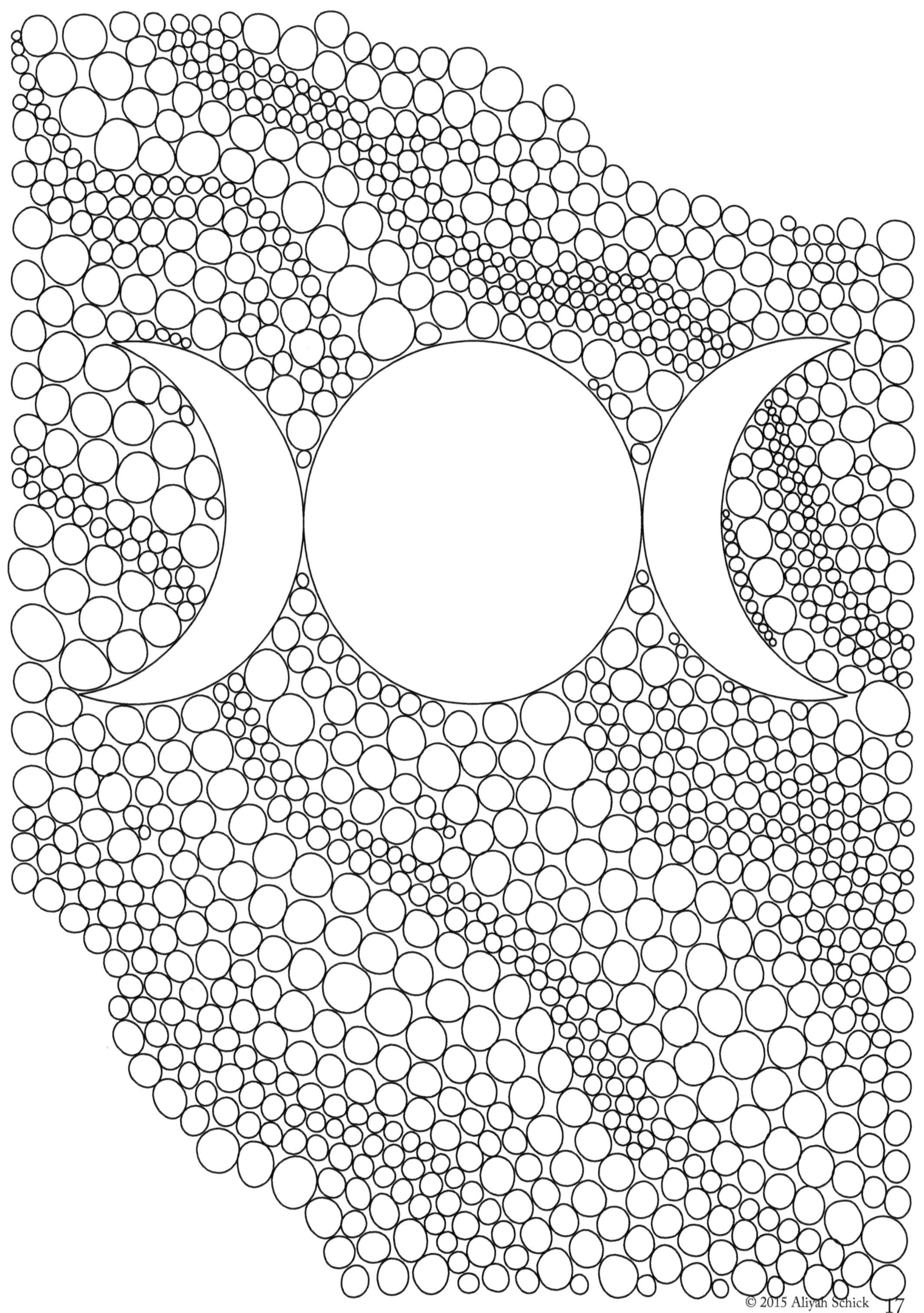

Meditative Impressions

Meditative Impressions

Meditative Impressions

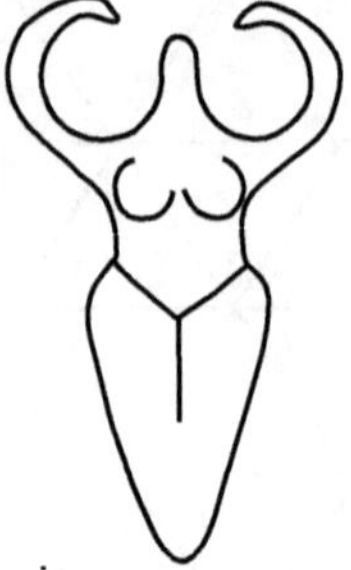

Meditative Impressions

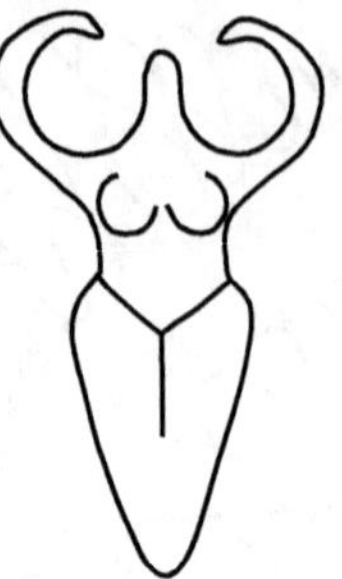

Meditative Impressions

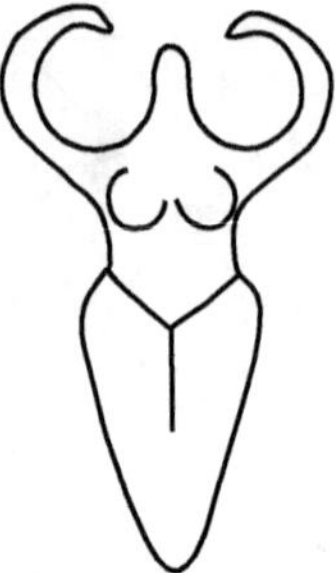

Meditative Impressions

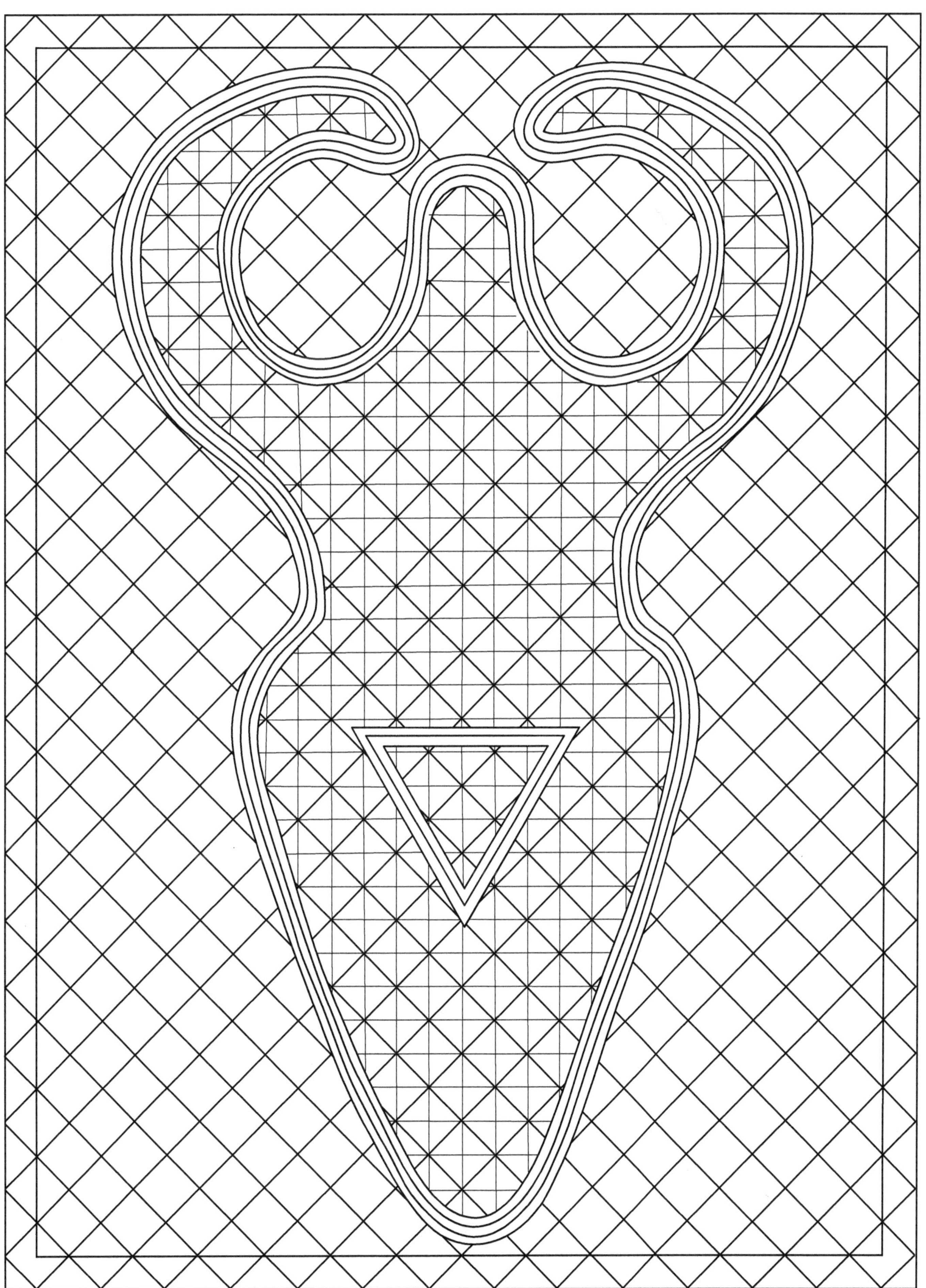

Meditative Impressions

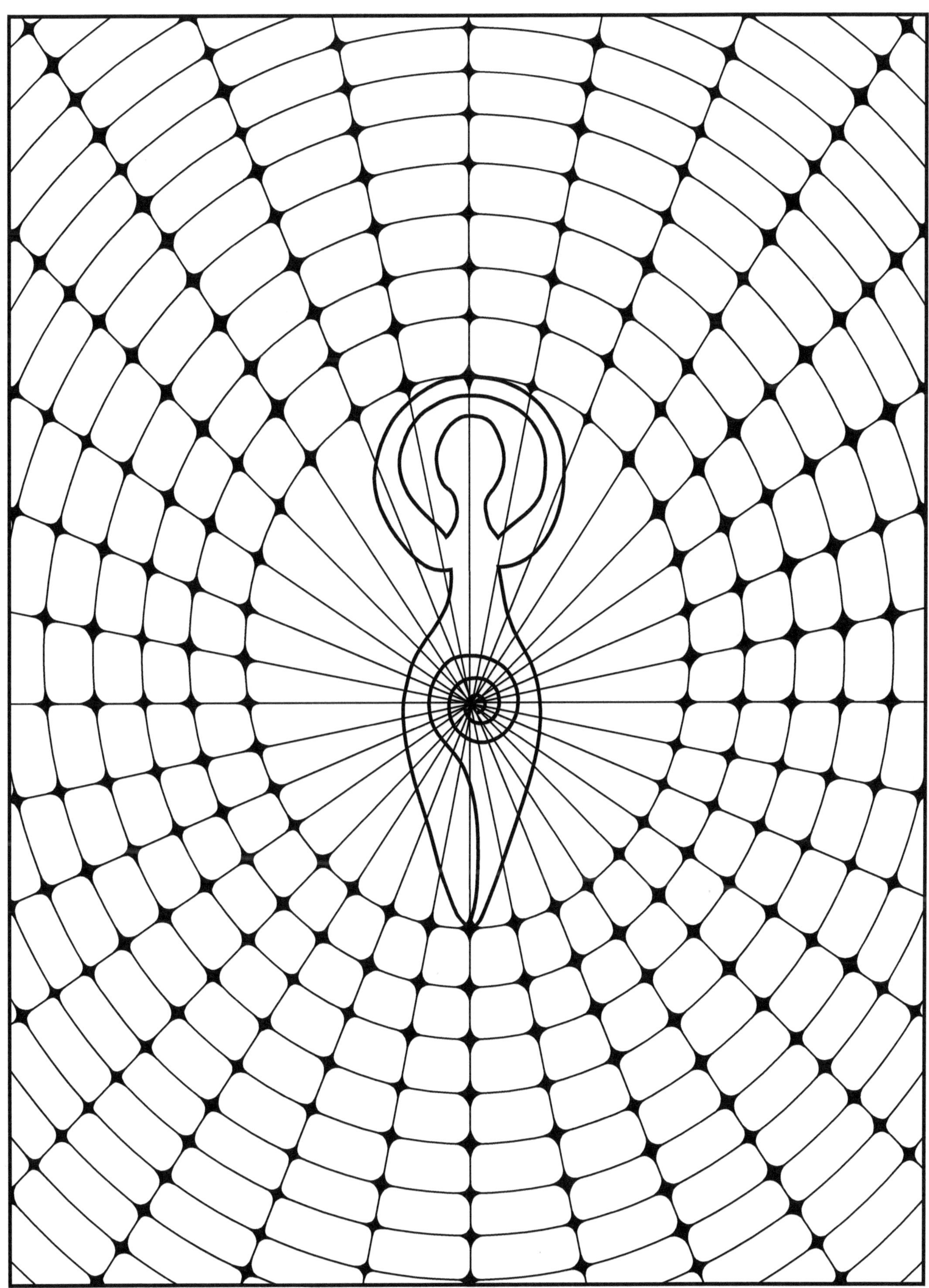

Meditative Impressions

Meditative Impressions

Meditative Impressions

Meditative Impressions

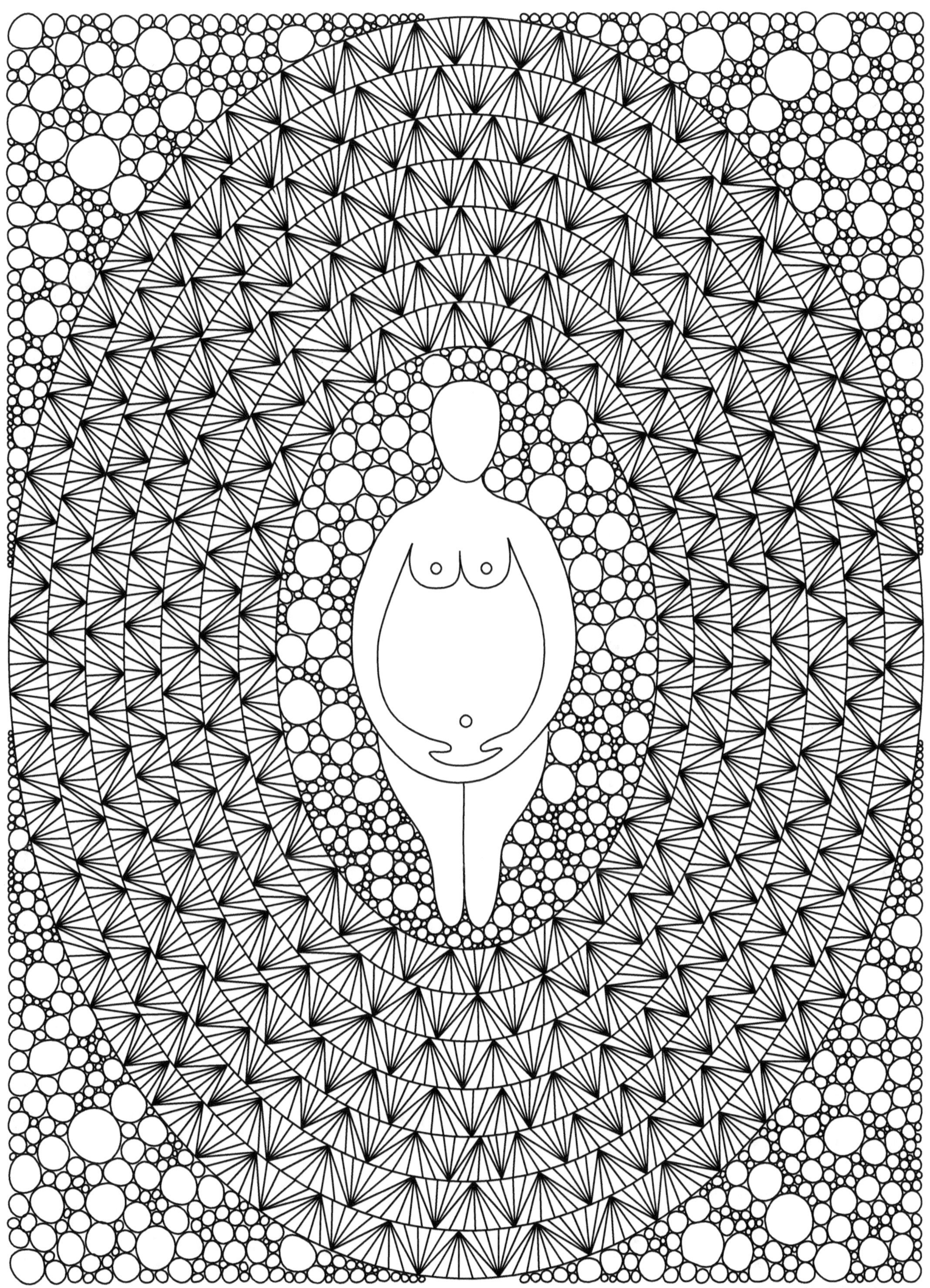

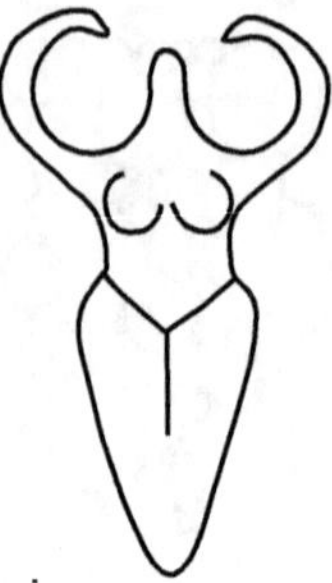

Meditative Impressions

Meditative Impressions

Meditative Impressions

Meditative Impressions

Persephone

KALI Innana

Aphrodite

Brigid ISHTAR

Demeter

Rhiannon Gaia

Artemis Diana

ISIS TIAMAT

HECATE LAKSHMI

Meditative Impressions

Meditative Impressions

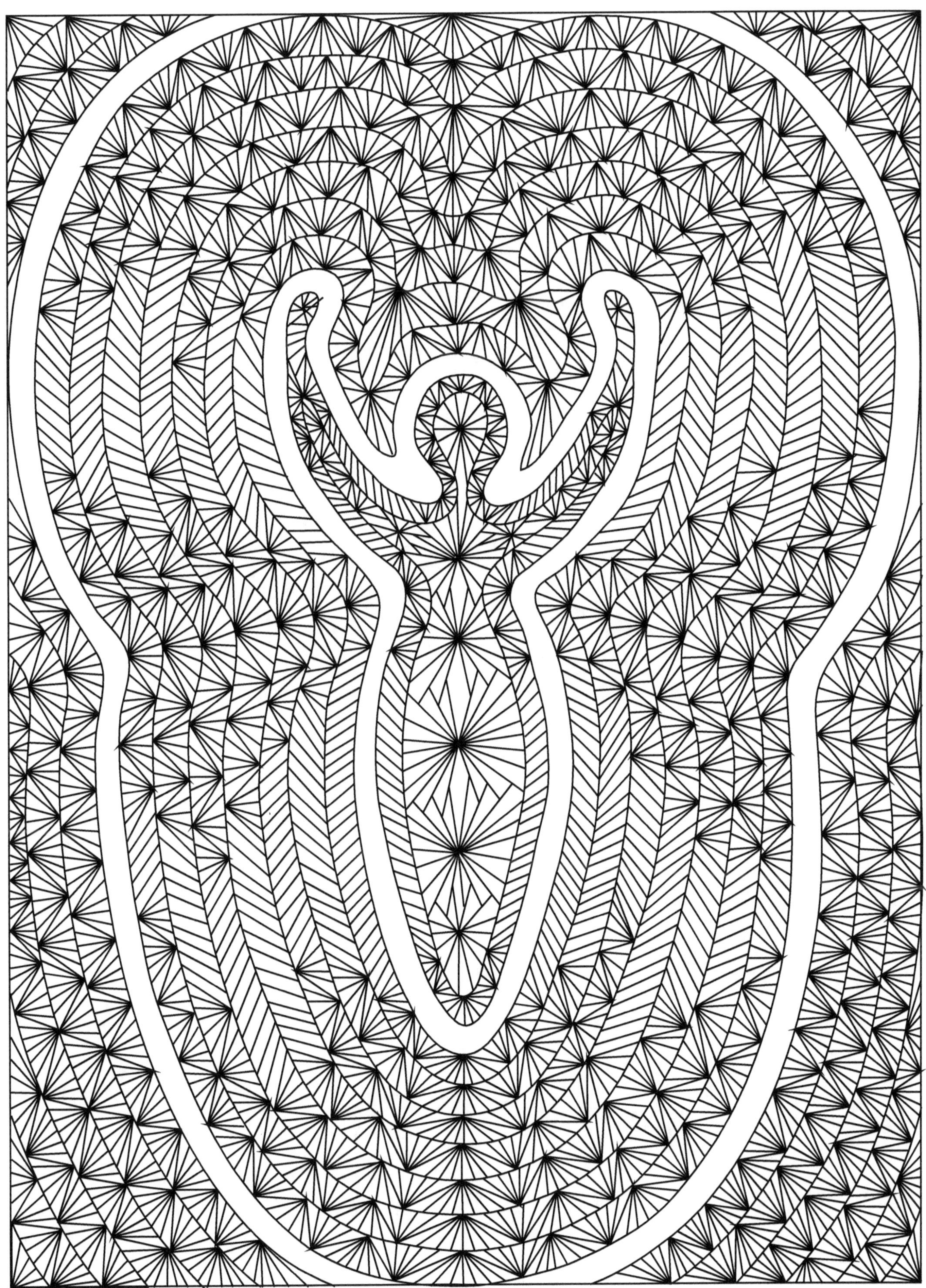

Meditative Impressions

Meditative Impressions

Meditative Impressions

Meditative Impressions

Meditative Impressions

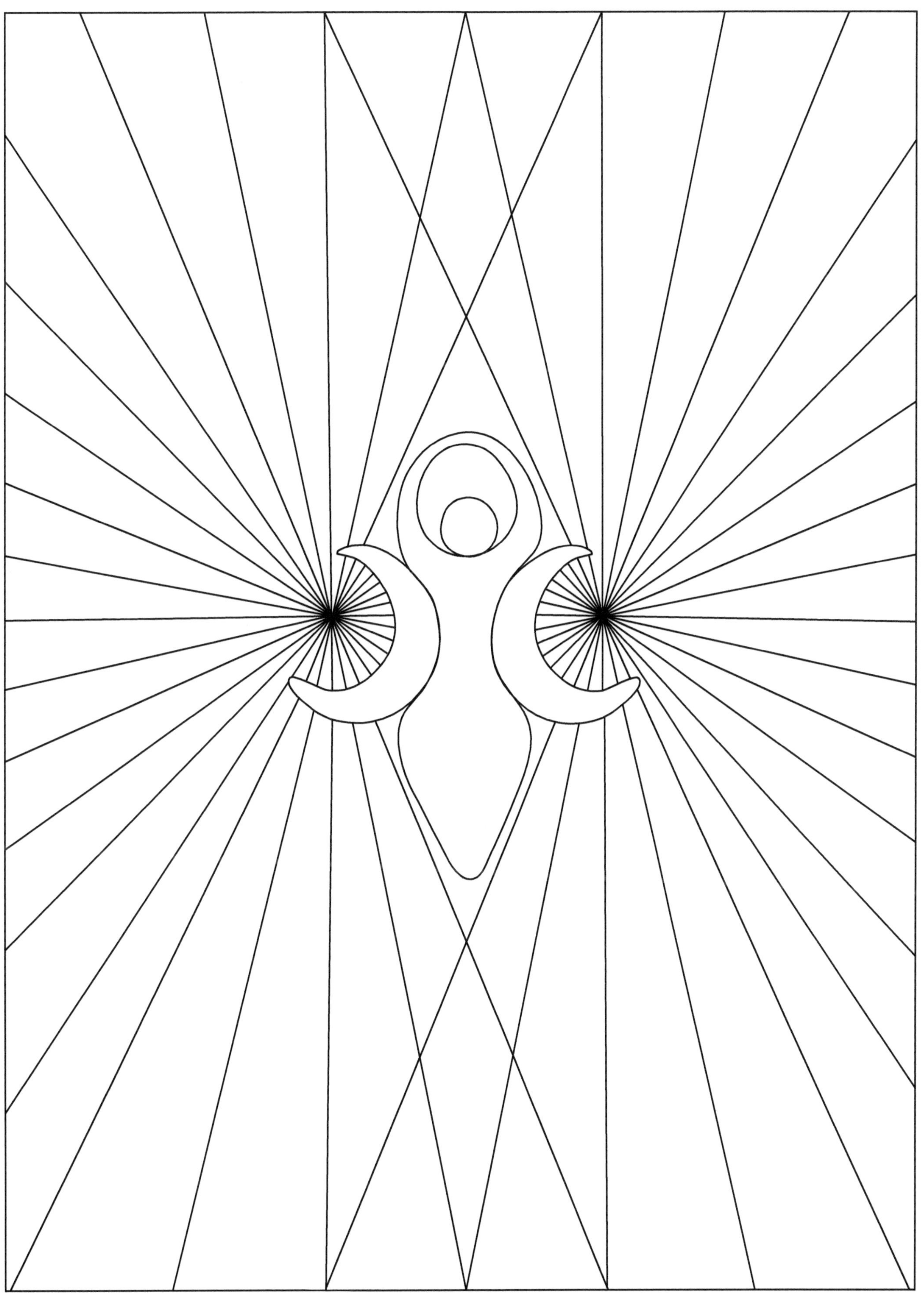

Meditative Impressions

Meditative Impressions

Meditative Impressions

Meditative Impressions

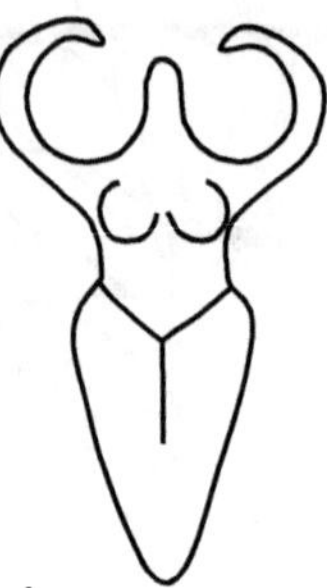

Meditative Impressions

Meditative Impressions

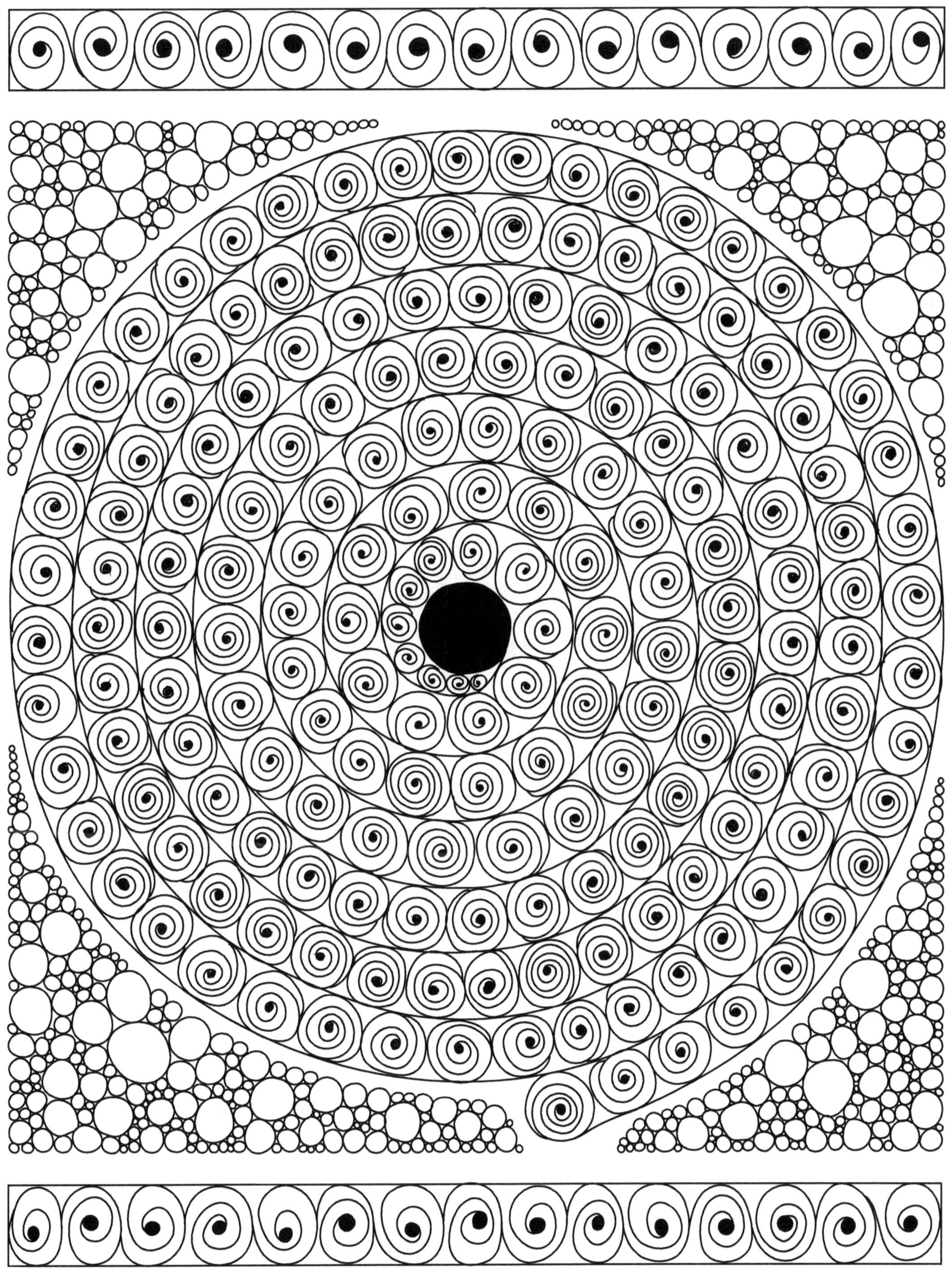

Meditative Impressions

Meditative Impressions

Meditative Impressions

Meditative Impressions

Meditative Impressions

Meditative Impressions

The Meditative Coloring Books Series: Angels, Crosses, Ancient Symbols, Hearts, Labyrinths, OM, and Goddess

Meditative Coloring Book 1 -- Angels

These angelic images are drawn with a pen in each hand, as artist Aliyah Schick allows the lines to go where they will, mirroring each other. Every movement is guided by spirit; every drawing is different; and each one is a wonderful surprise filled with angelic presence. Immerse yourself in the angelic realm as you color these drawings. Invite the angels to come into your world, to love and support you in all you do.

Meditative Coloring Book 2 -- Crosses

The cross is one of the most ancient and enduring sacred symbols, found in nearly every culture from cave dwellers throughout human existence. It symbolizes the celestial, spiritual divine coming into being in this material world. It represents the sacred taking form, and the integration of soul into physical life. These 36 original artist's drawings feature ancient and contemporary images of the cross in reflections of the deep spiritual significance of its form. Let the spirit and meaning of the cross fill you as you color these images.

Meditative Coloring Book 3 -- Ancient Symbols

Ancient and indigenous sacred images speak deeply to us, to our bellies and our bones, to our cellular memory and our wisdom, to our souls' yearnings. Native peoples throughout time and place see the sacred in all of life. For them, holiness is life and life is holiness. Life is the manifestation of the holy in all things. These original artist's drawings feature timeless designs used by every culture on earth to remind us of the sacred. Dip into deeply meaningful realms as you color these drawings.

Meditative Coloring Book 4 -- Hearts

The heart is one of our favorite symbols, evoking feelings of love, caring, loyalty, and devotion. As you spend time with these heart drawings, open your heart to live with more compassion for others and for yourself. Open your life to deeper connection with the earth and all of life. Open yourself to recognize the sacred in all things, including in yourself.

Meditative Coloring Book 5 -- Labyrinths

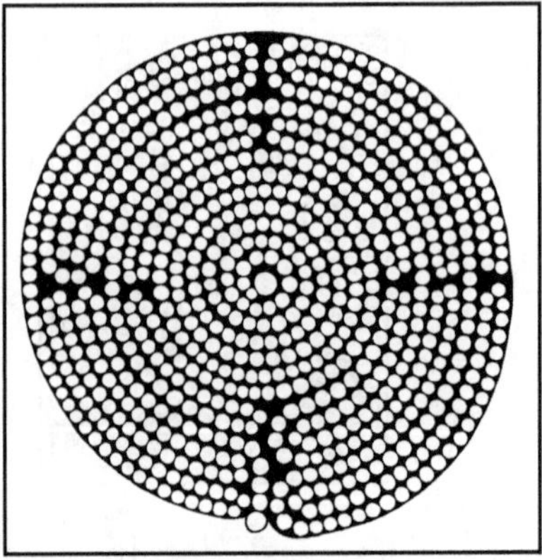

Color your steps into the labyrinth as you contemplate, meditate, or pray. Go deep into your inner wisdom and guidance where questions' answers reveal themselves and choices come clear. Or, simply relax and be with your breathing. Now you can bring your labyrinth with you to wherever you need to be. This collection of 36 original artist's drawings invites you into the labyrinth any time you wish.

Meditative Coloring Book 6 -- OM

Spend meditative time with the *OM* as you color these 36 original artist's drawings. Allow the *OM* to infuse and entune your spirit, your mind, your emotions, and every cell of your body with its pure, sacred grace. Fill yourself with its light. Become one with its beauty. Emerge relaxed, centered, calm, and at peace.

Color for relaxation, stress reduction, meditation, spiritual connection, prayer, centering, and healing. Color to calm and come into balance, to find your intuitive wisdom, and to learn to be more of your deep, true self.

www.MeditativeColoring.com

Meditative Coloring Book 7 -- Goddess

For 30,000 years in prehistoric time people all over the world celebrated and worshipped the sacred feminine. The Great Mother Goddess was the creator of all life and the life force within all life. Worship was every day here and now, holistic, visceral and sensual, all about earth, body, and nature.

Now we are seeing a revival of the sacred feminine through valuing nature, simplicity, mindfulness, meaningfulness, and clarity, along with a growing desire to honor intuition, right-brain knowing, and deep connection.

Color these 36 original artist's drawings as you open yourself to the sacred feminine in you. Nurture this long-abandoned side of conscious living, and bring yourself to a more sustainable balance.

The Labyrinth Guided Journal, a Year in the Labyrinth

The twists and turns of the labyrinth remove you from ordinary life, and draw you deeper into willingness, into yourself, and into sacred wisdom. Use *The Labyrinth Guided Journal* on your own journey through the next year. Each week the journal offers a new thought or experience or challenge drawn from the labyrinth, and a question or suggestion for you to consider and write about throughout the week.

The Jewish Coloring Books for Grown Ups

Color for stress relaxation, Jewish meditation, Shabbat peace, and healing.

JUDAICA Coloring Book

Menorah, dredel, Ten Commandment tablets, challah, Torah scrolls, Magen David, Havdalah braid, mezuzah, and more. Color these beautiful, original artist's drawings based on familiar Jewish objects and symbols. Relax, unwind, de-stress, and allow healing as you ground yourself into your Jewish heritage. L'chaim!

ALEFBET Coloring Book

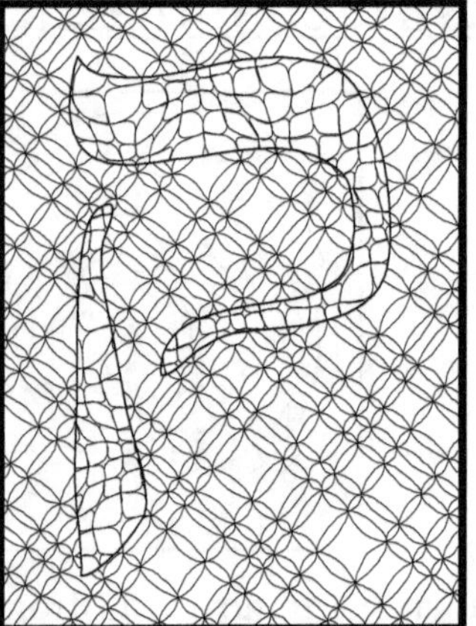

Alef, bet, gimel, dalet, hey, vav, zayin, chet, tet, yod, kaf, lamed, mem, nun, samech, ayin, peh, tsade, qof, resh, shin, and tav; 22 letters in the Hebrew alefbet. Coloring these 36 beautiful, original artist's drawings based on the Hebrew letter forms is relaxing, reduces stress, and lightens your load as it connects you with your Jewish roots. If these letters are the building blocks of the universe, then spending peaceful time coloring them can be beneficial in deeply healing ways, too.

CHAI Coloring Book

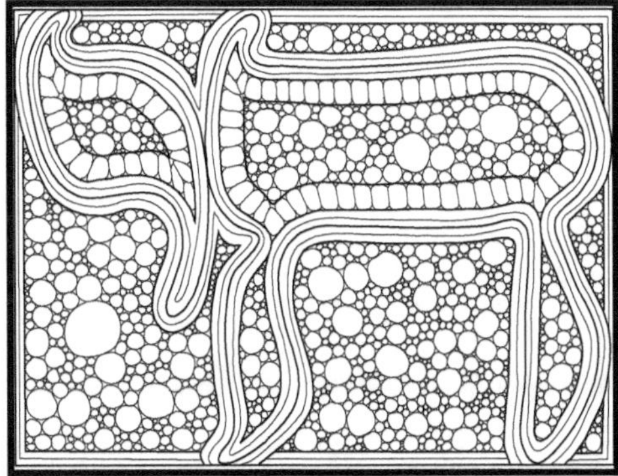

The Jewish *Chai* symbol represents the Hebrew word *chai*, meaning life. It is worn, displayed, or given as a gift as a symbol and reminder of the Jewish love for life, to celebrate being Jewish, and to bring abundant good luck. Spend relaxed, meditative time immersed in the many joys of the *Chai* as you color these 36 beautiful drawings.

STAR OF DAVID Coloring Book

The six-pointed Star of David is our most familiar Jewish symbol. Used as decoration and adornment on both religious and secular items, the Star of David represents Jewish pride in shared heritage, community, and family, and a declaration of hope and commitment. Spend time coloring these 36 original artist's drawings based on the Star of David and allow yourself to ground into your Jewish roots and celebrate your love of being Jewish.

Sacred
Imprints

www.ingramcontent.com/pod-product-compliance
Lightning Source LLC
LaVergne TN
LVHW081319060426
835509LV00015B/1595